NATIONAL STATUTES AND THE
LOCAL COMMUNITY

Local Taxation

National Legislation and the Problems of Enforcement

J. V. Beckett
Lecturer in History, University of Nottingham

Published for the
STANDING CONFERENCE FOR LOCAL HISTORY
by the
BEDFORD SQUARE PRESS of the
National Council for Voluntary Organisations

© SCLH 1980
ISBN 0 7199 1030 7

First published 1980 by the
BEDFORD SQUARE PRESS of the
National Council for Voluntary Organisations
(formerly The National Council of Social Service)
26 Bedford Square London WC1B 3HU

Printed in England by Henry Ling Ltd, at the Dorset Press, Dorchester, Dorset.

Contents

Foreword

This book is one of a series being produced by the Standing Conference for Local History about specific statutes, and describing the situation prior to the enactment of those Acts of Parliament, the manner in which they were enforced, the implications for local communities of the time, and the documentary evidence available to the local historian of today.

The series is under the joint honorary editorship of Mr J. J. Bagley, MA, FRHistSoc, formerly Reader in History, Institute of Extension Studies, University of Liverpool, and Mrs Jennifer Kermode, BA, Research Lecturer in the Departments of Medieval and Modern History, University of Liverpool.

The exercise of their editorial role calls for knowledge, understanding, and a willingness to contribute—in whatever measure may be required—from their resources of time and energy. Gratitude is expressed to them for their work, and to the author of this particular title for the preparation of his material.

Introduction

Until the nineteenth century local taxation was assessed and collected by traditional and haphazard procedures, and bore little relationship to the wealth of the country. It was assessed and collected by unpaid, and often inactive, officials. Amateur administrators did not relish contentious taxation procedures, and sought means by which to assess and collect local rates which did not normally include regular reassessments, or even efforts to tax on the legally required form of each man according to his ability. 'Ability' (i.e. income) was the standard imposed by the 1601 Poor Law Act. The services of paid officials were required to implement this Act, for the ratebook needed regular updating, and standardised forms of rating were necessary to ensure parity in the parish-by-parish taxation structure which was established by the Act. In practice, previous customary procedures prevailed in the localities, and land was the usual basis employed for levying a rate. The poor rate, for example (indeed most 'ability' taxes prior to 1799), quickly came to be levied by traditional means, usually based on real property. Whatever the law may have said, the poor rate became the basis of taxation at parish, county and even national level. Since it was seldom fully assessed in the parish, both because of abuses, and the failure to update rate books, this necessarily affected county and national taxes, and ensured that the taxable capacity of the country was neither known, nor realistically tapped. Only with Pitt's Income Tax of 1799 was an effective means of taxing by 'ability' found. Under these circumstances it is hardly surprising that local taxation functioned, or malfunctioned on an inadequate basis.

Despite various government-inspired reports during the nineteenth century, no Victorian administration was prepared to undertake the badly needed reform of the structure of local taxation. Consequently, whilst there is no one piece of legislation which can be highlighted as crucial for the history of local taxation during that century, the Act singled out in this book—that of 1815—was perhaps the most significant.

The purpose of the 1815 Act was to sweep away the traditional antiquated procedures, and to replace them with a system of local taxation in which the use of real annual property values would ensure equal rating between individual and individual, and between parish and parish. It was the first real attack on the problems of local taxation, although earlier statutory measures, such as the 1601 Act and the County Rates Act of 1739, were ineffectual government attempts to come to terms with the difficulties. Government inertia ensured the continuance into the twentieth century of the problems revealed in the aftermath of the 1815 Act.

I The Principles and Practice of Local Taxation to 1815

Local facilities in medieval England were maintained by an *ad hoc* system of benevolent munificence coupled with day labour. Not surprisingly a form of local taxation was developed to supersede such unsatisfactory arrangements, and as early as 1250 a rate was imposed at Romney Marsh to pay for repairs to the sea wall.[1] The 'fifteenths' and 'tenths', a national tax on land and movables, became the first truly recognizable local rate when the assessments were fixed on quotas in 1334, but local taxation only began to develop in a systematic way during the sixteenth century when legislation divided responsibility into two areas: the parish, which was charged with relieving its poor and maintaining its church and highways, and the county, which was entrusted with responsibility for repairing bridges, building gaols, relieving poor prisoners, and paying for the conveyance of rogues and vagabonds. By the early nineteenth century two major anomalies had developed in the structure of local taxation which the Act of 1815 was designed to counter. Firstly, almost all local rates, and some national taxes, had become little more than appendages to the poor rate, and secondly, each division of a county contributed to county rates by traditional proportions which were unalterably fixed.

ASSESSING AND GATHERING THE POOR RATE

It was from the great Elizabethan poor law statute of 1601[2] that principles were derived for assessing and collecting local taxation which were to be adhered to for more than three hundred years. By this Act, relief of the poor was to be paid for by a local income tax levied in each parish on the real ability of the inhabitants to pay. The size of parishes in the northern counties made this method inappropriate, and chapels of ease had begun to organise their own rates in Lancashire before the law was amended by the Poor Law Act of 1662. This empowered the six northern counties, together with Cheshire and Derbyshire, to use townships or constablewicks as the unit of assessment, thereby effectively standardising practice throughout the country. Since the provision was voluntary, individual parishes wishing to implement it were left to petition quarter sessions. Thus the vestry at Bywell St Peter, in Northumberland, summoned a meeting of the inhabitants in 1719 to consider petitioning the magistrates to divide the parish into four for poor rate purposes. Perhaps this was an isolated case since, according to the county historian, it was the later eighteenth century before much advantage was taken of these provisions. By contrast, several Westmorland parishes had their poor rates split by sessions before the end of the seventeenth century. A reference in the 1662 Act to 'other counties' enabled areas outside of those stipulated to invoke the terms of the Act. Leek, in Staffordshire, for example, took advantage of this clause in 1711 to have its poor rate split.[3] To try and ensure that there was never an imbalance between the supply of money and the demand for relief, the 1601 Act provided the magistrates with power to levy a local rate on one parish in aid of another. There is evidence of this happening as late as 1690 at Lewes in Sussex, and it was still traditional practice for one small parish in Worcester to obtain a rate from its neighbours in the mid-nineteenth century, but in general the clause does not appear to have been widely implemented after the Restoration.[4]

The assessments were to be levied by the churchwardens and overseers, and anyone dissatisfied with their rating had the right of appeal to sessions. It was only when rates began to rise at the end of the seventeenth century that parliament realised the dangers of leaving the sole power of making a rate in the hands of churchwardens and overseers with only nominal control from the magistrates. Legislation in 1699 noted that:

> many inconveniences do daily arise in cities, towns corporate and parishes, where the inhabitants are very numerous, by reason of the unlimited powers of the overseers, churchwardens and overseers of the poor, who do frequently, upon frivolous pretences (but chiefly for their own private ends) give relief to what persons and number they think fit.

The Act ordered the parish officers to keep a record of all persons relieved, and also permitted parishioners to give evidence against them in cases of embezzlement. Two Acts of 1744 were intended as a further check on their activities. By the first, churchwardens were instructed to give public notice in church of any rate for the relief of the poor so that each parishioner would know his contribution. The second ordered that all rates for poor relief should be entered in a book which would be open to public inspection. Abuses could not be entirely eliminated, and the case of Aspley Guise in Bedfordshire may not have been untypical. When a new assessment was made there in 1770 it was claimed that 'the overseer waited on [Francis Moore] to know what he would please to be tax'd at, he consented to 15s. per acre. They accordingly charged him as near to it as they could calculate.' From 1601 until 1801 the justices were only empowered to deal with cases brought by individuals, but in practice from the seventeenth century they had assumed the responsibility of ordering the form of assessment to be used in a parish. Even so it seems likely that many people endured what they considered to be unfair assessments rather than undertake the trouble and expense of an appeal.[5]

PROBLEMS OF EQUITABLE ASSESSMENTS

The poor rate was levied by the churchwardens and overseers who were:

> to raise weekly or otherwise by taxation of every inhabitant, parson, vicar and other, and of every occupier of lands, houses, tithes impropriate, propriations of tithes, coal mines, or saleable underwoods, in the said parish, in such competent sum or sums of money as they shall think fit. (cl. I)

However anxious they may have been to obey the letter of the law, the parish officials soon found that there was an anomaly in the 1601 legislation which made this difficult, if not impossible. By implication the Act included non-resident occupiers amongst those liable to contribute, and so produced a contradictory situation no one seems to have foreseen: how could the inhabitant and the non-resident occupier be coupled together in a system of taxation by 'ability' when it was inequitable for a man to be taxed in two parishes on the basis of his total ability? In the immediate circumstances of the seventeenth century this difficulty was resolved by a compromise; a man was rated according to the ability he possessed in each parish which, for all practical purposes, meant his real property. As a result there was a rigid separation of parishes which the legislators had not envisaged.

Whether or not this situation came about by accident, there is little doubt about the practical advantages of using land and property as the basis of assessment. In the first place such assessments were much less contentious than a tax on ability. As two justices found at Harborough in Warwickshire in 1632, 'the quietest and equallest way of levy was to tax every man according to his land and not according to estimation'.[6] There were many problems attached to assessing personal property and stock-in-trade, and it was always anomalous that only coal mines and saleable underwoods should have been included in the 1601 Act, rather than all mines and timber. The difficulty of assessing artifacts was well known to seventeenth-century hearth tax and eighteenth-century window tax collectors, who incurred antipathy from disrespectful householders as they went about their business. Even if the allegations of brutality have been exaggerated there is little doubt that such surveys were widely and vehemently resented.[7] In fact the problems of rating ability generally outweighed the financial advantage to be tapped, except perhaps in urban areas. At Folkestone there was an 'Ability Tax', and at Bishop Stortford in Hertfordshire early in the seventeenth century there was 'a rate called the forty shilling rate . . . being a rate for all manner of town charges and thereby to tax every man by ability, not by land (in regard the town consisteth most of tradesmen who hold little or no lands in their hands)'. An attempt to overturn this custom in favour of 'a new manner of rating both by lands and ability too', was rejected by sessions in 1637. At Bedford in 1662 it was ordered that the cost of renewing the town charter should be met by a tax on every person deemed by the assessors 'of ability to contribute'.[8] Stock-in-trade continued to be included for rating purposes in the clothing districts of the south and west during the eighteenth century, and it was still taken into account as late as 1778 at Monkwearmouth. Ability lingered on in several London parishes, and in one, St. Mary's Whitechapel, continued until 1833. By contrast the poor rate in Manchester at the end of the eighteenth century omitted most of the new houses, the tolls, and personal property which was liable to inclusion. 'Ability' was only dropped as a legal requirement in 1840.[9]

The second advantage of using land and real property was that this was usually the basis for assessing local rates. In the absence of administrative control parishes could adapt their normal means of assessment to the requirements of the poor rate. There was a wide variety of customary procedures. At Studley in Warwickshire it was recorded in 1626 that there was an ancient custom whereby when taxes became due the minister of the church gave notice 'after the time of divine service to all parishioners there that they should meet at a day appointed ... in the parish church at Studley there to tax and assess every one of the said parishioners as the occasions should require'. In the Lake District village of Grasmere people 'nicked their taxes upon two sticks (like tallies) by which they have been collected time out of mind', and at neighbouring Applethwaite rates were assessed on the women of the parish in proportion to their marital status and residence. In the Leicestershire village of Wigston Magna local expenditure was met by a levy on yardlands, horses, cows and communicants. In 1632, for example, the church-wardens recorded that they had 'rec[ceived] of the parrish by a peny a communicante, tow pence a cow and xii^d a yardland for ye church, viii^d a yard land for mold catching and viii^d a yard land for feild keping 14^l 18^s 0½^d'. Thirty years later the petty constables raised money for 'townes business' after the manner of '1^s 4^d the yard land & 4^d a schore of Sheep & 2^d a Cowe'. Elsewhere fixed proportions were used. The parish of Brewood in Staffordshire had four divisions which contributed in proportion to individual 'lewns' (the term used for levies in Staffordshire and Shropshire), and within each division the various inhabitants had a long standing assessment.[10]

Most local tax customs were based upon land, and originally on its area rather than its value. At Norton in north Derbyshire it was agreed in 1576 that each landowner should pay to local and national assessments in proportion to the number of oxgangs he possessed in the parish. The oxgangs (parcels of arable land normally containing fifteen acres) were estimated 'after the measure of the church wall', and those who contributed to taxes were held to be 'named in the church wall'. A similar technique was still used at Morton in Derbyshire in 1698. The use of area—it was generally known as rating by the 'yardland'—took no account of how the land was employed. This was accepted while the rates were low, but when they began to rise the inequalities became more apparent. As a result quarter sessions started to resolve cases brought before it by ordering parishes to use a pound rate (or rent) which would tax the *income* from land. There were a series of instances of this nature in seventeenth-century Warwickshire, such as the case of Ladbroke where the justices recommended in 1638 that 'the most equal way for their levies there ought to be made and paid by the pound rent and not by the yard land'. At the 1655 Michaelmas sessions in Norfolk it was ordered that rates in Humbleyard and Shropham hundreds should for the future be levied by a pound rate. Twelve years later Somerset sessions ordered three justices 'to appoint persons in the parish of Milverton to make and settle pound rates within the borough of Milverton and the vills and tithings in the parish, which shall serve as a rule and guide for future rates'. Previously rates had been made 'very unequally'. Finally in the Kesteven division of Lincolnshire in 1695 it was 'ordered that all the assessments belonging to the parish of Ewarby be rated and assessed by the pound rent and not otherwise unless cause be shown to the contrary'.[11]

The pound rate was not the answer to every problem, and occasionally the traditional practices were reaffirmed. Nicholas Knight, high constable of Barlichway hundred in Warwickshire, was accused in 1636 of altering the manner of ancient levies and taxes in Claverdon, Rowington, Henley and Ullenhall, without the consent of justices. Sessions ordered that 'the ancient manner of the payment of the levies and taxations . . . shall continue as formerly the same have been accustomed'. At Trinity sessions 1674, the two Warwickshire hamlets of the Gloucestershire parish of Welford objected to being charged by a pound rent, and the justices ordered that the old means of levying should be used. In 1657, Northamptonshire sessions ordered that at Bugbroke taxes 'shall for the future there be made and levied according to law and ancient custom'.[12]

The major drawback of using a pound rate was that of establishing real property values. A pamphleteer of 1764 attacked its use on the grounds that unless the lands had been improved it was fairer to employ a valuation of the acreage because the old rates were made according to the nature and quality of land. The author argued that a pound rate did not necessarily overcome inequalities; some farms were underlet so that to tax according to rent was, in effect, to tax according to the landlord's judgement.[13] One way of overcoming this problem was to tax on the basis of the rack rent. By 1729 Ryton Woodside in County Durham collected its poor rate 'after the rate of twelve pence in the pound at rack rent'. There was widespread feeling, however, that the rack rent was no more equal than the pound rate because, since no allowance was made for the burden of repairs, it did not represent the value of the property. An acceptable definition of a 'pound rate' was only reached with the Parochial Assessments Act of 1836 which laid down that assessments were to be made upon the net annual value of the hereditaments rated:

> that is to say of the rent at which the same might reasonably be expected to let from year to year free of all usual tenants rates and taxes, and the tithe commutation rent charge, if any, and deducting therefrom the probable average annual cost of repairs, insurance, and other expenses, if any, necessary to maintain them in a state to command such rent.[14]

In all likelihood this represented the common practice in use by the early nineteenth century, but it did not finally resolve the matter. The 1836 legislation also introduced special quarter sessions to deal with rating disputes, thereby formalising a long established practice in many counties of appointing two or three justices to investigate a rating dispute rather than resolve the matter in full sessions.

The absence of central government control of local taxation, coupled with the difficulty of assessing by ability, enabled parishes to collect the poor rate on the basis of customary procedures if they so desired. Where there was contention the justices could intervene, and for parishes lacking an established form of tax collection the Act laid down guidelines they could follow when a poor rate eventually became necessary. Over time, poor relief emerged as the most burdensome commitment of the parish and it became convenient to levy other rates—church rates and highway rates—on the same basis.[15]

COLLECTION OF COUNTY AND NATIONAL TAXES

Convenience also led to poor law assessments being used for county and national taxation. Tudor Parliaments seldom specified how county rates* were to be levied. The County Gaols Act of 1532 was an exception in that it laid a rate in twenty-five counties on residents having land, tenements, rents and annuities or estates of

---

*The corporate towns exercised the same powers of rating as counties, and they can generally be taken as included in references to 'county rates' in this book.

inheritance of the 'clear yearly value of 40s and above', or being worth in moveable substance the 'clear yearly value of £20 or above'. Such people were to be taxed in proportion to the value of income derived from their property. More commonly, Acts referred simply to well-established custom and precedent, the guiding principle apparently being that rates should be assessed either according to the benefit derived by the ratepayer as a result of the expenditure, or by his 'ability' when more neutral issues (such as the building of county gaols) were involved. In the absence of specific guidelines, the parishes began to raise their contributions on the same basis as the poor rate, and this practice was formalised in 1739. Legislation passed that year stipulated, amongst other things, that the sums raised for county quotas were to be levied within the parishes as an extension of the poor rate. The churchwardens and overseers were required

> out of the money collected or to be collected for the relief of the poor . . . to pay to the high constables of the respective hundreds or divisions of the said counties, cities or liberties, the respective sum or sums of money so rated and assessed . . . at such times as the said justices . . . shall by their order in sessions direct.[16]

Parliament was also unwilling to lay down definite rules for the collection of national taxation. During the seventeenth century central government began to impose quota taxes by which each county was expected to collect a stipulated sum of money but given a free hand as to the method employed. Quotas were first used for ship money in the 1630s and later for the Commonwealth monthly assessments. Despite their association with these unpopular taxes, they were regularly used by the government to raise extraordinary taxation after the Restoration. Indeed, even when a pound rate was demanded, the way in which it was to be assessed was not always enquired into. Commissioners were instructed to direct assessors to proceed 'according to the most just and usual way of rates held and practiced'. Cheshire, Warwickshire, Yorkshire, Cumberland and Westmorland are known to have used customary divisions for raising various seventeenth century national assessments. The final triumph for necessity over efficiency came in 1698 when quotas were adopted for the land tax.[17]

National levies based on quotas could be apportioned through a county in the usual way, and levied in the parish as an extension of the poor rate. As a result, the different levels of taxation became integrated during the seventeenth century, as the case of the Leicestershire village of Wigston Magna illustrates. In 1662/3, the petty constables collected a total of £97 7s 2d on different levies, of which about two-thirds went to the national exchequer, one-sixth to the high constable for county expenses, and one-seventh was retained for 'townes business'. The only recorded distinction in the basis of assessment was that for constablewick business sheep and cows were rated in addition to yardlands. The extent to which taxation was integrated is of course difficult to estimate. It was probably hampered by the mere fact that the petty constables collected for county and national taxes, and the churchwardens and overseers for parish levies. Even so, the regulations introduced in 1739 were probably taken to apply to national as well as county taxes, thereby helping to obscure the distinction between a rate and a tax drawn by Edwin Cannan:

> In the case of a tax, the taxing authority decides that individuals shall make particular payments on particular occasions, and the aggregate sum it receives depends on how much these payments add up to. In the case of a rate, the taxing authority decides how much money it wants in the aggregate, and this amount is raised by apportioning the payment of it between the various ratepayers in accordance with some definite standard made for the occasion or already in existence.[18]

Whatever the overall picture, the point to be stressed is that if the basic unit of assessment (i.e. the parish) was not fully rated, then the under-valuations became progressively greater at county and national levels.

The quotas used for county, and sometimes national taxes, bore little or no relation to real property values, and dated in some cases from proportions first employed for the 'fifteenths' and 'tenths'. These were, according to the eighteenth-century historians of Cumberland and Westmorland, 'certain sums and proportions . . . fixed upon the several townships within the respective counties (in Edward III's reign) according whereunto the taxation hath constantly been made'. Proportions of a 'fifteenth' were regularly collected in Ipswich during the fifteenth century, and, as late as 1603, the Lancashire justices ordered that 'half of a fifteenth shall be collected in Blackburn hundred for the repair of Holles bridge'.[19] Evidence about these customary divisions is contained in a government report of 1832 which was compiled from returns made by the clerks of the peace.[20] By that time some counties had already lost all record of their old procedures, or else withheld the information for reasons which are no longer apparent. Even so, the report, together with material in county record offices, makes it clear that these customary apportionments were originally developed in order to avoid the necessity of frequently reassessing property values, because this was expensive to implement and the results were notoriously unrealistic. They can be divided into three main categories for the purpose of analysis, although similar characteristics outweigh the differences.

In the first category were those customs which were based on what had once been a real valuation. Each hundred, parish and township bore a proportion of the county total, and sums of money were levied by fractions or multiples of this. Hence if a parish bore the rate of £5 to a county total of £100, when a county rate of £500 was demanded the parish would contribute £25. The figure of £5 could also be a useful base for assessing within the parish. The relative values of the different properties might be split proportionally to the £5 and then multiples could easily be calculated for a tax such as the poor rate. Five of the northern counties—Northumberland, Durham, Yorkshire, Westmorland and Lancashire—had adopted the old sixteenth century subsidy assessment books. For other counties the basis of the apportionment is unknown, although it can be assumed that they were derived from very old valuations. In Cornwall the total sum divided through the county was £118 19s, while in Devon it was £827 3s 10½d, in Herefordshire £225, in Merioneth £637 13s 4d, in Radnor £109 18s 3¾d, and in Rutland just £24 17s 6d. Dorset fixed its total at £496 5s 0¼d in 1672.

The 'subsidy' was the main Tudor and early Stuart extraordinary tax. It was based on *Books of Rates* in which, from 1566, each landowner recorded the value of his property. The rates rapidly became ossified so that by 1737 in Westmorland, for example, lands 'which are collectively valued in the book of rates at £62 [are] reputed to be upwards of £3070 per annum'.[21] How the books were utilised for collecting county rates can be demonstrated from a simple example. To raise £100 through County Durham, the local justices divided this amount by the total in the book of rates (£1086 13s 10½d in the later seventeenth century) and expressed the ensuing rate (about 1s 10½d) as '1s 10½d in the pound according to the book of rates'. Thus in 1804 it was ordered that 'the sum of £1443 8s 4d being an assessment of £1 6s 8d in the pound according to the book of rates shall be and the same is hereby assessed upon the said county to answer all and every the ends and purposes mentioned and intended to be provided for . . .'. This complicated arithmetic was preferable to frequent reassessments. Counties drew up lists of what could be raised by levying any given sum according to the book of rates. To avoid fractions more could be raised than was strictly necessary and the surplus used for unexpected county expenditure.

Possibly the most complicated arrangement was in Lancashire where the book of rates had evolved from the fourteenth-century 'fifteenths' and 'tenths'. Local taxation in the seventeenth and eighteenth centuries was based on an elaborate reassessment dating from 1624 when the justices decided upon

> A true and perfect Booke of all Rates and taxacons concerning this countie off Lanc[aste]r verie necessarie and profitable for all gentlemen off accompt and maie serve for a perpetuall president to theme and theires for the perfect and quick assessing of the said countie or anie parte thereof with what somes then shall att anie time bee imposed upon the same as hereafter maie plainely appeare.

A series of six different rates was agreed upon: the subsidy and fifteenth, which related to assessments granted by parliament; the oxlay, a tax dating from 1583 to provide oxen for the king; the maimed soldiers' lay; the prisoners' lay, for the Marshalsay and Lancaster gaol; and the soldier or county lay. This was the most important of the six. It dated from 1588, although several parts of the county simply adopted their ratings to the 'fifteenth', and could be used 'either for the mustering armey and surmising of the souldiers for the kings majestys warrs or for the trained bands or for repairs of bridges or aney other use or purpose within the said countie'. The purpose of the 1624 reassessment was to standardise all these contributions by recording the liability of the different hundreds, and of each parish within them, to the different levies. Thus for the oxlay and the soldier lay the 'sums which shall be taxed upon the said countie' were to be divided into one hundred parts and split in the following manner:

Hundred	Oxlay		Soldier lay	
Salford	16·5 parts	or £16 10s	14 parts	or £14
Derby	26 „	„ £26	24 „	„ £24
Leyland	8 „	„ £8	9 „	„ £9
Amounderness	16·5 „	„ £16 10s	19 „	„ £19
Blackburn	16·5 „	„ £16 10s	18 „	„ £18
Lonsdale	16·5 „	„ £16 10s	16 „	„ £16
100	£100		100	£100

Townships within each hundred were similarly divided.[22] Derbyshire used a division which bore a close resemblance, with rates being levied by an ancient mode of so much per trained soldier. To show the proportions each hundred was rated with a certain number of trained soldiers.

Across the Pennines in Yorkshire the book of rates settled in 1595 was used until 1816. The basic division of the county for taxation purposes had an even longer pedigree because in 1595 'the three ridings agreed with the ancient proportions of 12 for the West Riding, 10 for the North Riding and 8 for the East Riding'. The ridings were further subdivided into wapentakes. As in Lancashire, a series of different rates were settled. One was 'for provision of beeves for his Majesties household', another for soldiers (levied by the interesting division of $40 : 33\frac{1}{3} : 26\frac{2}{3}$ from the West, North and East Ridings respectively), and one 'for the levying any number of men and sums of money'. The mathematics could become extraordinarily complicated: it is difficult to know, for example, how Pickering in the North Riding managed to contribute $6\frac{39}{60}$ to a levy of 300 soldiers, and $8\frac{3}{25}$ to 400.[23]

The second mode of tax assessment, the single sum apportionment, was operated in a similar fashion to the customs included in category one. In Cheshire the 'mize' was a fixed division through the county amounting to £329 19s. It was used as early as 1594 and may originally have been based on a subsidy assessment. Cumberland, Gloucestershire and Warwickshire apportioned the sum of £100, and the Lincolnshire division of Lindsey £500, between their various districts. Cumberland, the odd one out of the northern counties, called its mode of taxation the 'purvey'. This was a development from the old subsidy assessments and the contributions to purveyance demanded in 1617, and it was often referred to as the county's 'book of rates'. The sum of £100—representing one purvey, just as £329 19s equalled one mize in Cheshire—was divided between the wards, parishes and townships, and the county rates were levied in multiples or fractions of a purvey. The need to retain the round figure in these counties meant that one division's relief had to be another's burden, and Cheshire successfully kept the mize intact until 1821. Elaborate tables showing the contributions of each division to any given rate were published for several counties, including Cheshire and Norfolk. During the 1740s the proportions due from each hundred and parish in Norfolk to sums of £300, £450 and £600, were published. These had been updated by the early nineteenth century to £1200, £1800 and £2400, which is an indication of the growth of the county rate.[24]

The third mode of tax apportionment was the use of ancient scales of relative proportions whereby each division of a county contributed a fixed proportion to any sum raised. Although Warwickshire used a single sum division, the proportions were fixed on the basis that in any charge on the county 'Knighthow and Kington hundreds pay an equal half part against the other two hundreds of Hemlingford and Barlichway . . . Knighthow is to pay 5 for Kington's 4 and Hemlingford 5 for Barlichway's 4 .[25] References in the 1832 returns to a scale of relative proportions such as these can be found for Suffolk, Monmouthshire, the Holland district of Lincolnshire, Carmarthenshire, Glamorgan and Pembroke. It is possible that similar divisions were also used in Huntingdonshire, Nottinghamshire and Brecon.

Finally what of those counties not yet mentioned? Staffordshire and Devonshire raised county rates on the basis of land tax assessments, the latter's quota having been fixed in 1694.[26] Two Welsh counties, Denbigh and Flint, simply raised a county wide poor rate. Only ten counties employed property valuations and of those, six— Buckinghamshire, Cumberland, Kent, Leicestershire, Middlesex and Oxfordshire—were using valuations obtained as a result of private legislation. The other four were Bedfordshire, Surrey, Sussex and Montgomeryshire. In Bedfordshire the valuation totalled £139,584, and ½d in the pound produced a county rate of £290 16s. Multiples or fractions of this figure were used for local taxes thereafter. For the remaining counties little or no evidence was provided in 1832.

There is nothing to suggest that these apportionments were regularly reassessed. Changes were made in Westmorland's book of rates in 1635—subsequently confirmed in 1660—and 1693, but there were no further alterations. The County Durham book was reassessed in 1680 when the total was reduced from £7063 to £1087 (tacit admission perhaps that the subsidy book had been abandoned, although the name continued in use). By 1804, various adjustments had further reduced it to £1085. A similar reassessment apparently took place in Northumberland during the 1680s, and the county total by the early nineteenth century amounted to £594. In Yorkshire, apart from a general order at Pontefract sessions in 1662 restoring all rates in the West Riding to their 1641 levels, there is no evidence of changes prior to 1815.[27] Two counties—Devon and Staffordshire—changed their quotas for the land tax during the 1690s and thereafter used the new quotas for collecting county rates. A report of 1794 showed that local rates were based on land tax assessments in Manchester.[28] None of the four counties using property valuations fixed other than by private legislation were using figures of very recent date. In Surrey the valuation used prior to 1815 amounted to £287,721, but when a new one was made it totalled £1,528,710. Bedfordshire, Shropshire and Norfolk were using apportionments fixed in 1739.

Opposition to reassessments came from areas of a county which believed they stood to lose. A dispute in Yorkshire was precipitated by the decision to turn the land tax into a quota tax in 1698. When it was first instituted in 1693 this was a pound rate assessment on land, personal property and the income from government office. As a result, when the tax was turned into a quota after five years, some counties retained their 1693 assessment as stipulated in the legislation. Such was the case in Yorkshire. An attempt was made in 1698 to reintroduce 'the old book of rates', and a dispute ensued with the strongest objections coming from those parts of the North Riding which believed they stood to lose. The matter was finally resolved at Bradford in 1699 when it was decided to obey the letter of the law and collect three-quarters (on a 3s rate) of the 1693 assessment.[29]

THE ACT OF 1739

Even if a county wanted to change its quotas, between 1739 and 1815 this was not possible. The variety of different county rates which were imposed during the sixteenth and seventeenth centuries had to be separately assessed and collected. In itself this was administratively wasteful because the sums involved were often so small that it was impossible to assess the inhabitants properly. In some counties one rate was levied to cover all county expenditure. Both Cumberland and Westmorland, for example, had adopted such a procedure by the early eighteenth century. What complicated the situation elsewhere was the absence of specific legislation about levying some of the rates. This had opened the door to legal challenges to the justices' powers. In one notorious case in Middlesex much of the money raised for the repair of Brentford bridge was spent defending a legal suit about the levying of the rate. The exasperated Middlesex justices petitioned parliament in February 1739 for legislation which would clarify their position. The case had revealed the need for justices to have stronger enforcing powers, but it was also realised that administrative time and costs could be greatly reduced by amalgamating the various rates into one county rate. *An Act for the More Easy Assessing, Collecting and Levying of County Rates*, which passed in the spring of 1739, was intended to alleviate these difficulties.[30]

The preamble of the Act set out the problem:

> It is apparent that the manner and methods prescribed by the said several acts for collecting some of the said rates are impracticable, and sums charged on each parish in the respective divisions being so small, that they do not by an equal pound rate amount to more than a fractional part of a farthing in the pound on the several persons thereby rateable; and if possible to have been rated, the expense of assessing and collecting the same would have amounted to more than the sum rated.

This having been recognised the justices were given

> full power and authority, from time to time, to make one general rate or assessment for such sums of money as they in their discretions shall think sufficient to answer all and every the ends and purposes of the before recited acts, instead and in lieu of the several separate and distinct rates directed thereby to be made, levied and collected. (cl. I)

Thus far the situation had apparently been satisfactorily resolved. Several counties either confirmed their old rate divisions or compiled new ones. Bedfordshire, Shropshire and Norfolk settled new apportionments, and a detailed breakdown of the Hertfordshire divisions has survived from 1739. Cumberland made alterations to its purvey roll, and the 1739 Michaelmas sessions in Hampshire ordered that the justices living in and near Winchester should meet before the next sessions 'to consider of a method to make a regular general rate upon the county pursuant to the statute lately made'. A long entry in the Staffordshire Order Book for Michaelmas 1739 recorded that a single county rate would be levied thereafter in place of the various individual ones.[31]

However, in the process of solving one set of problems the Act created others. The new county rate was to be levied

> upon every town, parish or place within the respective limits of [the justices] commissions, in such proportions as any of the rates heretofore made in pursuance of the said several acts have been *usually assessed.* (cl. I)

This provision reinforced the powers given to justices in 1701 to assess each place in their county 'as they usually have been assessed' towards the repair of bridges. Whether or not it was intended, the two Acts between them deprived the justices of the power to alter proportions. From 1739 they were only authorised to hear appeals 'against such part of the rate only as may affect the parishes or places in which they serve their offices'. The courts interpreted the Act in such a way as to establish that the hundred by hundred and parish by parish divisions were now inviolable.

Why this was done is not at all clear. If it was intentional then it may have been in an attempt to relieve the justices of the acrimonious disputes to which they could offer no real solution. Local taxation was levied on internal parish assessments organised by some 15,000 independent valuation authorities. Undervaluation was an inevitable result, and sessions depended on figures provided by self-evidently biased groups to decide whether one undervalued parish was unfairly rated *vis-à-vis* another. Difficulties of this nature make it reasonable to assume that in most cases proportions had been fixed for a long time, and thus the possibility of them being invalidated by fundamental alterations was not foreseen. Before 1739 there was some room for manoeuvre; thereafter the proportions were not to be tampered with.

BOROUGH RATES

The county corporate boroughs were not touched by the county rate and their position before 1835 was confused. They had the power to levy an internal rate in place of contributing to the county rate. Legislation in 1784 and 1823 empowered them to raise a rate towards the cost of administering justice and for the erection and maintenance of gaols. Just how many places had the authority to levy a rate was uncertain. A government report of 1835 named eighty-eight places claiming exemption from the county rate, while according to the Webbs there were about 200 municipal corporations by 1833. Of these about half of those in towns with a population of more than 11,000, and a quarter of those in smaller towns (*c.*50–60 altogether) were levying rates of one sort or another. Various levies in Lincoln during the eighteenth century were based on an ancient assessment of the parish and raised in multiples of £30 0s 7d. This valuation was more than a century old when a new one was made in 1830. York used the same valuation from 1740 until 1824. Canterbury's first rate, in 1773, was of 1d in the pound, while Newcastle upon Tyne's (in 1795) was paid out of the poor rate. The practice of meeting municipal expenditure by charging it on the overseers was widespread. At Huntingdon, for example, 'the gaol expenses are paid out of the poor's rates under the head constable's disbursements', and the Liverpool council engaged the poor law authorities to collect special rates marked down for particular purposes.[32] Some towns operated a borough-wide poor relief scheme, but the legality of this was doubtful and a number of private Acts were passed in the 1690s and again from 1749 to establish local independence. Thus legislation of 1770 united the Southampton parishes for the poor rate, and an Act of 1783 established a board of guardians for the parish of Birmingham. Towns such as Southampton managed without a borough rate for most of the eighteenth century, but this was usually only possible where there was a substantial borough fund.[33]

There was considerable opposition to any attempt by the unreformed corporations to extend their powers of rating. When new municipal expenditure was envisaged a separate authority had to be set up. Thus the Liverpool council established a body of watch commissioners in 1748 to guard and light the streets at night. An Act of 1815 to rebuild Bristol gaol established a body of gaol commissioners, and by 1835 there were several distinct tax levying authorities in the town. Not surprisingly there was friction between them and the corporation, and on occasion this could become acute hostility. Bristol's difficulties stemmed from the fact that within the ancient city there were seventeen parishes, some of them of microscopic proportions, and the resulting boundary anomalies produced a variety of rating problems and massive evasions. In theory Manchester's position was even more difficult because it was unincorporated and relied upon its court leet, which had no control over tax revenue. The town was not incorporated until 1838 and the court leet was only dissolved in 1846. In practice, however, an apparently unique 'town lay' was collected from the mid-sixteenth century until it was merged with the poor rate in 1778.[34] Despite these examples most towns found some convenient means of levying money to meet their expenses prior to the 1835 reforms.

THE INCREASING NEED FOR TAX REFORM

Although it was convenient to use real property as the basis of the poor rate, and the poor rate as the means of assessing most taxes, the evolution of such a situation was a reflection of the attitude adopted by central government towards the localities prior to the nineteenth century. Local government was run on the cheap, and since local officials were required to collect national taxation, it was in the interests of central government to tolerate inefficiency, and to avoid contentious direct taxation. Instances of government powerlessness are not difficult to find. Few people in the seventeenth century, for example, believed that the real taxable capacity of the country was being tapped. Charles D'Avenant was one who thought that the land tax would have yielded fifty per cent more than it did in the 1690s had real values been utilised.[35] The Staffordshire poll tax commissioners were reprimanded in 1667 for 'the partiality or non-observance of the true intention of the acts of poll'. For the land tax, money collected should have been remitted to London within twenty days, but the problems of slow collection and of finding ways to send the money led the board of taxes to allow the impression to take root that it was acceptable for the receivers to keep half a year's receipt in hand. By the 1790s this had been extended to a practice whereby the board informed receivers each year how much of their balance was to be paid off, and the counties were circulated in 1798 to discover the procedures they used for collecting the tax. Disregard for the law could be even more blatant. The window tax was collected as an ordinary county rate in Cumberland

and Westmorland from the time it was instituted in 1696, but when the abuse came to light in 1713, and efforts were made to rectify it, Cumberland MP James Lowther was told by the Lord Treasurer that 'we might be easy whatever was given out or pretended'. According to another local landowning MP, Sir Christopher Musgrave, even the poll taxes were converted into a county rate in Cumberland during the 1690s. This idea was considered in Westmorland but, after some deliberation, rejected.[36] Political blind spots such as these were necessary on the part of central government given the prevailing philosophy of non-intervention and economy in local taxation affairs, but such lack of interest was a licence for maladministration.

Whilst it was content to rely on an inefficient local administration, central government was powerless to introduce an efficient system of direct taxation under its own control, and so by-passed the issue on the occasions when it arose. The inability of Elizabeth and the early Stuarts to 'live of their own' was an open invitation to reform, but instead of accepting the challenge, the government introduced a new indirect tax, the excise. From the 1690s the financial requirements of prolonged continental warfare presented another opportunity for reform, but politicians tried to manage on unpopular measures such as the land tax. In an attempt to curry favour with the landed gentry, Walpole tried to replace this with additional excises in the 1730s, and when it proved incapable of producing the necessary revenue by the 1770s, Lord North turned to a further series of assessed taxes. Even Adam Smith, whilst disliking indirect taxes, hesitated to promote the obvious alternative and lent support to a compromise, the house tax. William Pitt reverted to assessed taxes when the French wars broke out in the 1790s, and when he finally bowed to the need for income tax the move was thoroughly detested. The first opportunity was taken to dispense with it when the war ended, and it was not until 1842 that income tax was finally introduced as a permanent peace time tax.[37]

The reluctance of central government to put its own house in order makes it hardly surprising that the localities were allowed to develop an inefficient system of their own which could be converted to most purposes. Almost by accident most local and some national taxation was based upon rates laid on the annual income derived from visible property within the parish in which a tax was levied. Although it worked this was an inadequate system. The first major government report on local taxation in 1843 concluded that the provisions of the 1601 Act were 'all very rudely done', but lip-service was paid to the principles of the Elizabethan statute throughout the nineteenth century, and they were not finally laid to rest until 1925.

By the turn of the nineteenth century it was clear that the old structure of local taxation was seriously inadequate. With the whole weight of local, and in some cases national, taxation placed on the parish-by-parish poor rate, and county taxes levied by fixed proportions, it is hardly surprising that the system was incapable of adapting to the changing social and economic circumstances of a rapidly industrialising nation. There was growing resentment of the way in which assessments fell exclusively on land and real property when these were losing their central position as realistic tax guides. A contributor to the *Gentleman's Magazine* had complained in 1744 that farmers paid the great burden of the poor rate just as they did the land tax. Houses, he claimed, were severely underrated, while land was left to the mercy of parish officers anxious to reduce their own commitment by not having to collect from too many different places. Potential tenants of farms were demanding that the landlord should covenant to pay the poor rate because of the great burden it placed upon them. Twenty years later, a plan to mend the roads for which no turnpike trusts existed by raising an assessment rather than using the traditional statute labour was opposed on the grounds that 'this proposed assessment will be an additional land tax and fall ultimately upon the landlord'.[38] Industrialisation brought its own difficulties which highlighted the general failure to tax 'ability'. Mills and factories were not difficult to include within a pound rate, but canals and railways were a new problem because they passed through several parishes and yet operated on the collection of tolls payable at the termini. Even more serious was the position of the extractive industries. Only coal mines were specifically mentioned in the 1601 Act and other mines were held to be exempt from rating because they were specualtive and often loss-making. Not surprisingly there was considerable disquiet that as mining generally became more profitable many ventures were untouched by taxation.

If industrialisation was one problem enclosure was another. Within the parish it was usually possible to secure acceptable revaluations after an enclosure and sessions would normally adjudicate in the few disputed cases. In 1638 at Bourton and Draycott in Warwickshire the inhabitants consulted the justices when they differed over whether to use yardlands or true yearly value as the basis of assessment because 'every yardland of the lands enclosed are worth £25 per annum and the yardlands lying in the common fields not worth above £10 per annum'. A decade later at Warmington newly enclosed lands were worth £12 a year and those in the common field only £8, which produced a request to sessions for permission to use a pound rate. Compromises were even arrived at during the time of parliamentary enclosure in the eighteenth century. An agreement was reached at Aspley Guise, in Bedfordshire, in 1761 that, because of the cost involved, the local assessments should remain static for the next twenty years. When efforts were made in 1770 to reassess, Richard How opposed the chief promoter of this agitation, Francis Moor, on the grounds that it was common practice to fix a time period during which no reassessment should take place.[39]

Whilst the parishes could keep abreast with changes in values, the provisions of 1739 were a millstone around the counties' necks. Enclosure altered the relative taxable position of a parish *vis-à-vis* its neighbours, yet this could not be reflected in county rates. The clerk of the peace in Flint commented in 1832 that several thousand acres of the county had been enclosed, but no additional tax burden laid upon them. New housing was another improvement not reflected in county rates. A witness before the 1834 select committee on local rates described the position in Dorset where

> the rate has not been revised since the town of Weymouth has been built; therefore the town of Weymouth does not contribute a single 6d towards the payment of the county rate. There has been also upwards of 40 enclosure bills in the county of Dorset, which is not a large county, now there is not a single acre of the new lands enclosed under these bills which contributes towards the payment of the county rate, and therefore, necessarily, must make it more heavy upon the other ratepayers.

If this was the situation in an agricultural county then the anomalies must have been even more glaring in an industrial area such as Lancashire where no changes had been made since 1624.

Some counties had at least attempted to reflect town building in their county rates before 1739. In Westmorland the 1693 reassessment of the book of rates was mainly to give the growing town of Kendal a separate rating which it had not previously enjoyed. Cumberland's purvey was altered in 1701 to take account of the rapidly expanding port of Whitehaven. Changes of this nature were impossible after 1739. Gloucestershire clothier and justice of the peace, Sir George Onesiphorus Paul, based his complaint of 1803 that 'the ratio by which the county rate is levied is, of all others, the most inequitable', on the grounds that no account had been taken of housing improvements. He cited the case of Clifton parish in Bristol which 'covered as it now is, with magnificent houses, pays 3s 10d as it did almost two centuries ago when it was a bare common field, while the deserted manor of Sudeley still pays its 11s 0d as in the days of its splendour'.[40]

Parliamentary enclosure and urbanisation on the scale that they took place in the second half of the eighteenth century could hardly have been foreseen in 1739. Neither could the rise in the poor rate—from £2,004,238 in 1784 to £7,036,969 in 1832, and the county rate—from £315,805 to £784,771 between 1792 and 1832. These figures served to emphasise the inequalities and also to subject the administrative machinery of local taxation to an intolerable strain. A government report in 1834 blamed the increased county expenditure partly on the growing population, but more crucially on the rising cost of prosecuting suspected criminals and guarding proven offenders. From 1774 county executives started to build or rebuild their gaols and houses of correction. Such measures required high capital expenditure, but the money had to be collected by machinery geared to maintaining existing services in a stable and unchanging society, and not for raising large sums of money for new purposes. Local government was run by gratuitous personal service based on a substantially unaltered annual obligation, and as more money had to be collected from more people the traditional amateur administration gradually lost its ability to cope. As the Webbs concluded:

> the mere collection of the greatly swollen rates from thousands of shifting occupiers, to say nothing of the control of an expenditure which had risen to unexampled sums, involved, in itself, a transformation of the machinery of local government.

A few adaptations were made to the existing structure. High constables and county treasurers began to pay themselves small sums of money for services rendered, although this was actually illegal. But whilst it was clear that the whole machinery needed overhauling the task would have been difficult and perhaps impossible in the unreformed parliament.[41]

As a result desperate efforts were needed to fit the outdated procedures to the changed circumstances. The parishes could normally resolve their internal problems but the counties had to search for ways of circumventing the traditional apportionments. One means of doing this was to obtain a private Act authorising a pound rate on real property valuations when projects involving considerable capital expenditure were involved. Two Acts in 1809 allowed County Durham and Northumberland respectively to build a new gaol and a moothall, and both stipulated that a pound rate should be used to raise the finance.[42] A second means was for a county to obtain legislation enabling its justices to levy an equal rate for all purposes. Middlesex led the way in 1797, and was followed by Leicestershire in 1804, Kent in 1807, Cumberland in 1810, Oxfordshire in 1813 and Buckinghamshire in 1814. The motive behind Cumberland's decision to seek legislation was the need to raise money for building the new courts of justice at Carlisle, while in Kent it was the search for an equitable way of paying for gaol upkeep. For certain local government purposes Kent had been recognised as consisting of two divisions—west and east—by an Act of 1732. When a new gaol was built at Maidstone in 1746 West Kent bore the whole cost. From 1793 however there was agitation to have its upkeep borne by the county as a whole, and an Act of 1803 repealed the 1732 legislation in favour of having common county expenses apportioned throughout the county. The Kent Equalisation Act of 1807 retained the formal unity of the county and empowered the justices to make a fair and equal county rate.[43]

Private Acts required internal county agreement, but there were many people who believed it was not in their best interests to have the rate equalised. Devon provides a good example of the contention which could arise. Two parishes believed themselves to be so disproportionately rated by 1810 that they petitioned sessions for a reassessment. Inevitably this was refused by the justices on the grounds they did not have the power to make such a change. As a result an association called 'The Promoters of a New and Equal County Rate' was formed in the autumn of 1811, to try and persuade the parishes most heavily burdened by the existing rate of the need for a new one. Lists of the parishes supporting reform began to appear in the local press, and several parishes petitioned parliament in January 1812 for legislation to equalise the rate. Their argument was that the quotas, fixed 118 years previously, were now 'enormously disproportioned'. Leave was given to bring in a bill, and this was accordingly introduced in February. A series of petitions were presented against it and the bill got no further than a first reading. At Michaelmas sessions 1812, a proposal to seek a new rate was negatived by the decisive majority of 31 to 6, a decision which prompted three justices to condemn the action of the majority in the *Exeter Flying Post*. At the same time a correspondent of the *Gentleman's Magazine* claimed that the Devon rates had risen from £827 (the total for a single rate) to £30,000 a year in the course of sixty years.

> and the disproportions on parishes vary from one to 260 degrees; added to which, there are sixteen valuable parishes not charged, besides various extra-parochial places, and out of 450, of which the county consists, 300 are rated beyond par; and not any two can be said to be fairly rated, each paying too much or too little.

In December 1812 three petitions were presented to the Commons asking for leave to bring in a bill to equalise the Devon county rate, and as a result a bill was read for the first time in February 1813. There followed a series of petitions for and against the bill—there were at least fifty-six against—and it was eventually lost in April 1813. The opposition was led by Lord Rolle, one of Devon's half dozen really substantial landowners at this time, and he had the backing of seventy magistrates. Consequently, despite the inequalities —some of which were highlighted in an article published by the *Exeter Flying Post* of 12 November 1812—nothing further was done in the county before 1815.[44]

II The Act of 1815

It was both expensive and a drain on parliamentary time for
each county to apply for an Act, while Devon's experience revealed
how wealthy interest groups could frustrate reform efforts. If
parliament was deaf to calls for a complete reform of the structure
of local taxation, then a general Act to allow the counties to abandon
their stereotyped divisions and to sweep away traditional practices
in favour of an equal pound rate was the next best thing. Agitation
for such a measure began early in the nineteenth century. There is
no official record of any attempt being made to meet the complaints
in 1802, although the annual vestry of the parochial chapel of St
Nicholas and Our Lady in Liverpool was told of a bill 'now before
parliament' to equalise the county rate. Its parish committee had
petitioned against the bill because if it passed in the form proposed
'a very heavy burden would have been cast upon the parish at large,
by an annual rate for the service of the county on the full annual
value of all real property lying within it'. Liverpool corporation
had also objected and it was hoped that the town would be exempted
from the bill's provisions, because borough interests were funda-
mentally different from those of the counties.[45] A contributor to
the *Gentleman's Magazine* in 1810 complained bitterly about the
inability of the justices to alter existing parish proportions. It was,
he argued, 'a business deserving the attention of parliament'.
Parliament responded in a small way in 1812 with legislation to
amend the 1739 Act in relation to county bridges.[46]

One drawback to reform was the cost to each county of revaluing
itself in order to use an equal pound rate, but this was less of an
obstacle once the property tax returns were available from 1803.
Addington's Property and Income Tax, introduced that year, and
Lord Henry Petty's similar measure between 1806 and 1815, stipulated that returns were to be made of income from particular sources.
Owners of land, including houses, were taxed under Schedule A,
and because these returns were taxed at the point where the income
first arose, they provided accurate lists of valuations. This information was used in Leicestershire, where the justices made a rate
in accordance with the 1804 returns, and Buckinghamshire.[47]

The agitation for reform, coupled with the precedent set in 1812 and a readily available means of valuation, paved the way for a general Act. A bill was introduced into the Commons during the summer of 1814 to ease the assessing, collecting and levying of county rates. This failed for want of time, but it was quickly followed the next session by a similar measure which was successful. *An Act to Amend an Act of His late Majesty King George the Second, for the More Easy Assessing, Collecting, and Levying of County Rates*[48] received the Royal Assent on 12 May 1815. It was claimed that this was merely an extension of the 1739 legislation which had been made necessary because 'the laws now in force are found ineffectual for the correction of the disproportions which now exist, or which may from time to time take place, in the assessment of county rates'. In fact the Act was rather more significant than its title suggests. Its purpose was twofold; first it was to sweep away customary apportionments, and secondly it ordered that local taxes should for the future be levied on the true annual value of property liable to the poor rate, which was to be the basis for distributing the charge between and within parishes.

In its own words the Act was to empower the justices

> whenever circumstances shall appear to require it to order and direct a fair and equal county rate to be made . . . to assess and tax every parish, township, and other place, whether parochial or extra-parochial, within the respective limits of their commissions, rateably and equally, according to a certain pound rate (to be from time to time fixed and publically declared by such justices), of the full and fair annual value of the messuages, lands, tenements, and hereditaments, rateable to the relief of the poor therein, any law or statute to the contrary thereof notwithstanding. (cl. I)

They were further 'authorised and empowered' to require the constables, churchwardens and overseers of the poor, assessors and collectors

> to make returns in writing to the justices of their respective divisions in petty sessions assembled . . . of the total amount of the full and fair annual value of the several estates and rateable property within the parish, township or place, whether parochial or otherwise, to which they respectively belong, charged or assessed to the poors rate, at the time of making such return, or liable to be, or charged or assessed on any other rate or assessment, whether parochial or public, without regard nevertheless to the actual amounts or sums

assessed on the property therein, save and except in such parishes, townships, or places only, where such property is assessed to the full and fair estimated annual productive value. (cl. II)

Having admitted that the existing provisions were inadequate, the Act was laying down regulations aimed at producing a fair and equal assessment within and between parishes. There was provision for future reassessments so that the existing stalemate could not reoccur (cl. XII), and counties which had reformed themselves by private legislation could do so again under the terms of this legislation. (cl. XXI)

III How the Act of 1815 was Implemented

The intentions of the men who framed the legislation of 1815 were admirable. Here, in theory, was a major piece of legislation sweeping away the traditions of centuries; but in practice things were rather different. The title of the Act reveals that its real purpose was to tackle a perceived grievance arising from the 1739 legislation, while its terms show that it was framed in ignorance of the true state of local taxation. One result was that three amending Acts were required over the next six years: to sort out doubts concerning the contributions from extra-parochial places, to amend the proceedings in cases of appeal, and to specify the position of parishes and townships which straddled county borders.[49] These were relatively minor difficulties by comparison with the other failings of the Act: it was not compulsory, it was not sufficiently specific about revaluations, and it strengthened rather than removed the motives for undervaluation.

The provisions of the Act were voluntary and the following list shows how each county took advantage of them in its own good time.

Counties revalued by private legislation prior to 1815

1797	Middlesex	1807	Kent	1813	Oxfordshire
1804	Leicestershire	1810	Cumberland	1814	Buckinghamshire

Counties revaluing under the terms of the 1815 Act

1815   Lancashire, Lincolnshire (Holland, Kesteven districts), Yorkshire (East Riding), Monmouthshire
1816   Derbyshire, Devon, Essex, Surrey, Sussex (West and East), Warwickshire, Westmorland
1817   Huntingdonshire, Worcestershire, Yorkshire (West Riding)
1818   Nottinghamshire, Somerset, Staffordshire, Wiltshire
1819   Herefordshire
1821   Cheshire, Hampshire
1822   Berkshire, Lincolnshire (Lindsey division)
1823   Durham
1824   Hertfordshire, Yorkshire (North Riding)
1825   Gloucestershire
1826   Glamorgan
1827   Cambridgeshire, Montgomeryshire
1829   Caernarvonshire
1830   Northumberland
Before 1832   Anglesey

Counties unchanged in 1832

Bedfordshire	Rutland	Carmarthen
Cornwall	Shropshire	Denbigh
Dorset	Suffolk (East and West)	Flint
Norfolk	Brecon	Merioneth
Northamptonshire	Cardigan	Pembroke
		Radnor

Eighteen counties used property tax assessments as the basis for reform, five revalued on the basis of rack rents, ten on annual value, two on actual value, and the final six on a variation of the poor rate valuation.[50]

Among the counties quick to take advantage of the Act was Lancashire, which had the most glaring inequalities. At the general sessions on 29 June 1815 the county's justices ordered 'a fair and equal county rate' to be made. The property tax collectors were to make returns to the justices in petty sessions of the 'annual value of the several estates and taxable property within each parish, township or place charged or assessed in the assessment for the duties on property under schedule A for the last year'. The Warwickshire justices were not slow to order a new valuation, and when it was completed in 1816 a 1d rate yielded £4,887 16s 8d. Westmorland sessions waited until 1816 before resolving to levy a new county rate based on the average sums assessed in the four wards for the property tax. It was completed in May 1818.[51]

The voluntary nature of the legislation meant that it was little help to the Devon reformers. The same opponents of a private bill now resisted efforts to implement the Act's terms in the county, despite several petitions—mainly from the rural areas—to sessions in 1815. The parish of Washford Pyne, for example, claimed that its assessment of 14s 7½d would be reduced to 7s 2d in an equalisation, and so begged the magistrates 'to proceed immediately to exercise the powers vested in them by an act passed in the last session of parliament'. At the January sessions in 1816 Viscount Ebrington, champion of the reformers, and Lord Rolle engaged in a dispute which was only terminated when the lord lieutenant intervened on the side of reform. With 111 of the 513 parishes in the county actively supporting the call for a new rate, one was made in time to be introduced at the Michaelmas sessions that year.[52]

Why did so many counties, especially in Wales, ignore the Act? There is evidence of obstinacy on the part of justices, which suggests

that some counties may have been subject to the same sort of power-
ful interests which nearly prevented change in Devon. Others
clearly did not regard their inequalities as sufficiently disproportionate
to warrant a revaluation. This was certainly the case in Northumberland which was valued in 1809 for building the moothall, and
again between 1821 and 1824 for meeting the cost of a new gaol, a
house of correction and a sessions house. Despite these valuations
the old book of rates was not superseded for raising the normal
county expenditure until 1830. It seems likely that some of the
Welsh counties were as unconvinced as Northumberland about the
need to revalue. Elsewhere the cost proved to be prohibitive. At
any level reassessment could be a financial encumbrance. Members
of the vestry at Gnosall in Staffordshire found this when they
agreed in 1790 that because the poor rate was irregular and disproportionate a land surveyor, Samuel Wyatt, should be employed
to make a fresh valuation and assessment. It cost £100. Multiplied
onto a county level such figures could have serious implications. A
Dorset magistrate, the Rev. H. F. Yeatman, told a government
enquiry of 1835 that he presented three petitions to quarter sessions
in April 1823, all arguing the case for a reassessment. Nothing had
been done by the time the matter was raised again in 1830, by which
time the existing rates had been more or less unaltered for 158 years.
When tenders were sought the lowest was £13,324, and rather than
pay such a sum the inequalities were bearable. Fortunately a solution to the problem of cost had been found by the 1830s. The
Lancashire reassessment of 1815 was quickly outdated by the
industrial development of the county, and following an appeal
from Liverpool, a new one was ordered in 1829. A scheme using
averages was adopted which enabled the survey to be completed
in the space of seventy days at a cost of only £917. The parish
officers were ordered to make a return of 'the actual rent and value
of lands, farms, buildings and tithes . . . the mills, factories, bleach-
works and print-works, canal properties and railways'. This done,
'a certain number of instances of each description of property were
selected . . . and then a calculation was made on the supposition . . .
of what the description of property ought to be'. The West Riding
of Yorkshire was on the verge of following this example in 1834
when a government select committee was sufficiently impressed
to recommend that in counties which had not revalued since 1820
'a new valuation should take place, in the mode adopted by the

county of Lancaster', or under a similar scheme which was proposed for Dorset.[53]

The case of Lancashire illustrates a second problem arising from the voluntary nature of the Act: the need for regular revaluations. Social and economic changes in nineteenth-century England rapidly outdated assessments and all the old inequalities could quickly reappear. The 1815 Act allowed the justices to make a new rate whenever circumstances appeared to require one, but with no property and income tax returns after 1816, revaluations were less easy. Gloucestershire relied upon these figures when it made the change in 1825, even though they must have been at least ten years out of date by then. The much sought after Devon revaluation was already 'exceedingly unequal' by 1834, and the government report of that year recommended revaluations at least once every twenty-five years to ensure that the growing towns would contribute in due proportion 'so far to relieve the landed property and the farming tenantry from the undue pressure of the county rate'. In 1836 it was believed that only nine counties had revalued in the previous seven years, in eight the existing valuation could not be found, and in a further five it was about one hundred years old. The example of Middlesex, where there were frequent reassessments from 1797, was not followed elsewhere, and the 1834 report concluded that nearly twenty years after the Act 'the valuation upon which the county rate is levied varies extremely in different counties . . . and bears with unequal pressure on different parts of the county'.[54]

The final failing of the 1815 Act was that it both strengthened the motivation for a parish to undervalue itself, and did nothing to ensure that the 1601 principle of 'ability' was enforced. No change was made in the manner of assessment and collection. Responsibility remained with the justices, churchwardens and overseers, and the only concession to their increased responsibilities was a provision empowering the justices to compensate those involved for the time and energy they spent on rating and collection. As long as internal valuations were relied upon, it was inevitable that parish officers would do all they could to ensure that it looked as if the capacity of their parish to contribute to the county rate was much less than that of their neighbours. From 1739 it was common practice to find the true value and then reduce everyone's contribution by anything up to a half or even three-quarters. The motive was reinforced by the provision of the 1815 Act that the poor rate should continue to be the basis of all rates, and although it was partially offset by the additional power given to justices to enquire into the validity of a valuation, the overseers were hardly encouraged to go to any great lengths to find real values. This failure to ensure proper valuations was repeated in the Parochial Assessments Act of 1836 which was actually intended to prevent the practice of undervaluing. Yet again, however, this was a voluntary measure, so that a parish not reassessing itself continued to enjoy the old advantages.

REFORMS OF THE 1830's AND BEYOND

The mistakes of 1815 were largely a result of ignorance about the existing situation, and things had changed very little when the reform ministry began to take an active interest in local government affairs during the 1830s. The rising level of local expenditure had become a matter of serious concern. A royal commission was set up to try and establish, among other things, what had caused the poor rate to rise by 251 per cent in the half-century prior to 1832, and there was similar concern about the 148 per cent rise in the county rate. Returns from the counties in 1832 had revealed the unpalatable fact that the 1815 Act had not been an immediate success. This prompted the government to appoint a select committee to investigate the working of the Act, and to suggest regulations which might diminish the pressure of local rates on the owners and occupiers of land. The committee found that certain charges—for prisons, prosecutions and inland transportation—were of national importance and general utility so that they were really the responsibility of central government. A parallel investigation under the auspices of the House of Lords, and yet another committee in 1836, reached similar conclusions.[55]

These findings were not altogether unexpected; a report of 1825 had suggested the need for grants-in-aid. The difference in the 1830s was that because of its desire to supervise local affairs central government acted on the recommendations, and imperial grants became an established feature of relations between London and the localities thereafter. The various reports revealed the inadequacy of central government knowledge, and the result was an investigation by the poor law commissioners into the whole structure of local taxation. Their report was completed in 1843 and revealed a sorry mess. They found that there were more than 200 imperfectly defined purposes for which twenty-four different rates could be levied. In practice these were simply raised on the poor rate, although had the letter of the law been enforced many of them should have been assessed separately, while some, it was claimed, could not have been assessed at all. There were inconsistencies as to what property and which people should be rated and, because the legal checks to ensure that the law was put into practice were inadequate, neither the 1815 Act nor the Parochial Assessments Act of 1836 had done much to solve the problems. Furthermore the failure to reform the procedures of assessment and collection meant that there were no less than fifty-four different species of officer concerned with local taxation, and those simultaneously in office perhaps numbered 180,000 of whom by far the larger portion were annual officers.[56]

It was clear that piecemeal reforms such as the 1815 Act were inadequate. The commissioners proposed nothing short of a thorough reform of the structure of local taxation, involving 'numerous changes in the existing law', although they were careful to point out that none of their suggestions was necessarily dependent upon any of the others. There were three major recommendations. First, one general rate should be levied, on the basis of the poor rate, to replace the twenty-four existing taxes and to consolidate local taxation in much the same way as the 1739 Act had done. Secondly, rates should fall on all fixed, but not on movable, property. Finally, a professional system of valuation should be introduced as a way round the inadequacies of the 1815 and 1836 Acts. A brief examination of the fate of each of these proposals shows the reluctance of central government to undertake the necessary measure of reform.

In the second quarter of the nineteenth century the number of new local rates was on the increase. Normally they used the poor rate assessments but there was no uniformity of practice and a separate administration was created for each rate. An abortive attempt was made in 1850 to secure a system of valuation (see below) which would eventually have led to consolidation, and the need for a general rate was repeated by select committees in 1868 and 1870. The first of these suggested that the unnecessary trouble and expense of so many authorities and rates could be alleviated by levying an annual consolidated rate to be fixed at the beginning of each year. In the 1880s William Rathbone, a member of an old established and wealthy Liverpool family and an MP for the town, complained that there were still twenty-three different kinds of local taxation, and argued that a single rate would lay the foundations of a simple and intelligible system of local finance. It was to be another half century before this came about.[57]

The absence of uniformity was most apparent in the boroughs. The Municipal Corporations Act of 1835 abolished the customary rates and replaced them with a borough rate, but it did not create a single rate assessment for the borough. This was only possible where the borough and poor law union were coterminous, a situation which could be achieved by a provisional order or a private Act. At the turn of the twentieth century there was still a distinction between borough and poor rate, and, theoretically, different assessors and collectors for each. A further problem of overlapping jurisdictions, unsolved by the Act, related to the collection of rates. In Bristol, for example, the Incorporation of the Poor was the body responsible for the collection of the general rate, but while the city boundaries were substantially expanded in 1835, those of the Incorporation remained unaltered. The council sought clarifying legislation in the Small Tenements Act of 1837. This empowered the churchwardens, overseers of the poor and nominees of the Incorporation, to assess, strike and collect the rate in those areas joined to the city. In the older areas the task was left to the Incorporation. The problems were still not wholly overcome, and defaulting continued even after the Bristol Rates Act of 1845.[58] Finally the Municipal Corporations Act left open the problem of where borough ended and county began. As a result, towns such as Birmingham fought a running battle with the county around them, and the situation was not eased until legislation of 1849 'to provide a more convenient mode of levying and collecting . . . rates in parishes situated partly within and partly without the limits of boroughs which are liable to such rates'.[59]

The second proposal of 1843 was to bring local taxation into line with practical reality by rating all fixed and no moveable property. The 1601 principle of 'ability' had never been successfully implemented, and indeed stock-in-trade was so seldom rated by the nineteenth century that it was ignored in the Parochial Assessments Act. In 1839, however, the court of Queen's Bench decided in the case of *The Queen* v. *Lumsdaine* that the 1836 Act had not put an end to the rating of personal property. The Poor Rate Exemption

Act of 1840 was passed to clarify the situation. This was commended in the 1843 report, but it was not until 1874 that legislation was enacted to include all mines and timber for rating purposes.[60] After 273 years rates finally came to be levied only on fixed property.

The poor law commissioners' proposals concerning valuation were the most difficult to implement. They recognised that because the poor rate was the basis of most other taxes, unless it was raised on a true valuation there would always be inequality. Yet even if the 1815 and 1836 Acts had been compulsory, it was unrealistic to expect a parish to adopt an expensive process which would serve to ensure that it was fully rated. The valuation officer needed to be disinterested as between individuals and parishes. This diagnosis was indisputable but it skirted the real issue of how valid it was to use the parish as the unit of taxation. The Poor Law Amendment Act of 1834 had attempted neither to reform the rating system, nor to find a more viable unit of relief. Though parishes were grouped into unions they remained responsible for the cost of relieving their own poor and the result could be grossly unfair distribution within the union. A witness before the 1850 House of Lords committee reiterated the familiar story that although assessments were reasonably accurate within the parishes, 'with reference to the comparison of one parish with another, I find the assessments extremely defective'. The 1850 committee was considering a bill designed to establish 'a uniform mode of rating for all rates, for entire counties including all towns and counties of boroughs'. Sir Cornewall Lewis, its sponsor, was hoping to see larger units established as a means of overcoming valuation anomalies and, eventually, to secure consolidation. The bill failed, but together with the committee report it highlighted what was becoming a major point of contention: the continued use of the parish as the unit of rate assessment. One proposal, put forward in 1849 by G. L. Hutchinson, was to replace the poor rate with a country wide local income tax of 1s 6d in the pound. This scheme was championed by the Earl of Malmesbury in evidence to the 1850 committee. He argued that it was clearly inequitable for all local rates to be levied on real property, and that the parochial system was inappropriate because it ensured that the urban parishes which had the most poor had to find the most money to support them. But Malmesbury's argument, that it was time to abandon the principles of 1601 because circumstances had changed radically since that time, was not yet a popular one.[61]

As yet reforms were limited to what could be achieved within the limits of the parish and there were some efforts in this direction during the 1860s. The 1862 Union Assessment Committee Act gave the boards of guardians greater control over the valuation of parishes, in an attempt to solve the problem of inequalities within the unions. Together with the Union Chargeability Act of 1865, it succeeded in providing for the revision of the valuations in the separate parishes by a committee responsible to the whole union. These measures neither solved the problem of obtaining uniformity of rating, nor prevented friction between the constituent units of the union. Already many areas which were dissatisfied with the rating system had obtained special powers through private legislation, while the 1862 measure was confined to the poor rate, and there was no provision for extending use of the valuation roll to other taxes collected on the same basis. [62]

A further attempt to promote uniformity came in 1867 with a bill which proposed a single assessment authority in each county, annual revisions of the valuation list, and a complete revaluation every three years. The bill was lost but there was one successful measure a couple of years later with the Valuation (Metropolis) Act of 1869. Legislation passed in 1856 had given London a consolidated rate, and the 1869 Act added uniform valuation practice and regular revaluations. Moreover, the valuation was to be made in conjunction with the Inland Revenue as a means of assimilating the basis of rates to the Schedule A returns. This apart, however, most of the efforts to bring about reform were unsuccessful despite the pioneer work of G. J. Goshen in the 1870s and the complaints of William Rathbone in the 1880s. The latter pointed out that the union could make one valuation, the county another, and the borough another; separate machinery could be used for collecting each rate, and a separate series of accounts could be drawn up for each. He regarded the need to rationalise local government affairs as a matter of urgency. The Royal Commission on Local Taxation, which produced five reports between 1899 and 1901, recommended that there should be one valuation authority for each county and one valuation list as the basis of all taxes. For all this effort the reforms did not come until 1925. [63]

The unsolved problem left two anomalies. First, the question of undervaluation remained open throughout the nineteenth century because the parish remained the unit of assessment and the overseer the assessor. Furthermore, the cost of valuations ensured that with no legal necessity to revise them little effort would be made by the parishes to do so. Second, no real attempt was made to sort out the burden of rates on different classes of property. The Lighting and Watching Act of 1833 introduced differential rating whereby houses and buildings were to pay a rate three times as high as agricultural land. Differential rating also provided an equitable means of assessing canals and railways in a parochial structure, but many other problems remained. Tithe owners were believed to be the only people fully rated to the poor rate, and the case for relieving them was presented before several select committees. Small tenements presented another difficulty. The structure of local taxation was not equipped for collecting minute amounts of money from vast numbers of individual properties. In some places, perhaps most notably Manchester during the 1790s, these properties were simply ignored. Legislation of 1819 enabled parishes to charge some landlords by a composition rate on property, but a variety of private Acts were passed to regulate the assessment of small tenements in particular places. The idea of owners being rated where the annual value of the property fell below a minimum sum was put forward in 1843. After a select committee recommended that the limit should be £6 in 1850, the suggestion was taken up in the Small Tenements Act of that year. This was another voluntary Act, and less than one in five West Riding parishes had instituted its terms by 1858. There was still considerable variety of practice a decade later, with some areas employing a minimum figure of £10. William Rathbone continued to believe that small ratepayers were disproportionately rated. 'Broadly speaking', he wrote in 1869, 'the percentage of his income that a man pays to the poor rates is often in the inverse ratio to the amount of his income. The wealthier he is the smaller the percentage he pays'.[64]

The recommendations of 1843 were only fully implemented with the Rating and Valuation Act of 1925,[65] which finally demolished the inadequate structure of local taxation. At long last the general rate was introduced, provision was made for quinquennial revaluations, the overseers were swept away, and the parish was replaced as the rating authority by county boroughs, boroughs, urban and rural districts. Nearly a century after agitation about the structure of local taxation had begun, and more than three hundred years after the great Elizabethan statute, the machinery of local rating was at last reformed. What the Elizabethans had seen as a system designed to raise small sums of money for local purposes by an assessment based on each person's 'ability' had evolved into the modern rating system. Perhaps not surprisingly there have been several further Acts since 1925. Today our rates are levied according to the terms of the General Rate Act of 1967, which was repeated in the 1974 Local Government Act. Local taxation has a long pedigree.

Taxation is an emotive issue which governments tackle with reluctance, as its history in England illustrates. A fundamental reform of national taxation was needed in the eighteenth century and of local rating in the nineteenth, but successive generations of politicians baulked the issues, merely scratching the surface with botched measures to meet short-term difficulties. Indeed the major taxation change during the nineteenth century was the divorce of local and national assessments. The Property and Income Tax enabled national taxes to take on a distinct form of their own, rather than being merely an appendage to local assessments. Yet herein lay a contradiction. The Valuation (Metropolis) Act of 1869 was the first attempt to use the Inland Revenue schedules for local taxation purposes, even though this was an obvious means of overcoming the problems of under-assessment. The characteristic tendency of English rating assessments to sag well below actual rents was only corrected towards the end of the century by using the Schedule A returns. This reluctance to take the necessary measures of reform, even after they were spelt out in the 1840s, was based on the need to obtain consent to taxation and helped to delay the fundamental reform of local rating until the twentieth century.

This being the case, why single out the 1815 Act for special attention? The importance of the Act was not so much in what it achieved as in what it revealed. It was designed to sweep away customary practices in favour of a new system of equal valuations throughout the parish and county, but its implementation was slow and haphazard, thereby revealing the inherent difficulty of dislodging the counties from their traditions, and highlighting the problems of trying to find true valuations. It also raised the question of how often reassessments were necessary in a rapidly changing society, and how they could be obtained. Thus, whilst in its terms and conditions the Act was not very important, it at least revealed the problems to be faced. Moreover, it was partial legislation, passed to meet a particular need in ignorance of the real situation. It might have been a very different measure had central government ordered a full investigation before legislating. Equally there might have been more significant reforms if the government had acted upon the various reports prepared during the 1830s and 1840s. The story of local taxation prior to the twentieth century, however, is one of continued avoidance of change. It is a history bound up with the principles of consent, in which central government allowed an inadequate and inefficient system to continue because it was not prepared to risk rocking the political boat by steering boldly into the turbulent waters of tax reform.

Source Material

Local taxation is an important aspect of the history of local government, because it throws considerable light on the tensions both within the various levels of local government, and between the localities and central government. Yet it has received surprisingly little attention from historians. Edwin Cannan's book, *The History of Local Rates in England*, which was first published in 1896, is still the basic text on the subject. Other works which make some reference to it include W. E. Tate, *The Parish Chest* (1946), J. Redlich and F. W. Hirst, *Local Government in England* (2 vols, 2nd edition, edited by B. Keith-Lucas, 1970), W. Holdsworth, *A History of English Law* (13 vols, 1922–52), and the various volumes of the Webbs' work on *English Local Government*. Dorothy Marshall, *The English Poor in the Eighteenth Century* (1926) and G. W. Oxley, *Poor Law Relief in England and Wales 1601–1834* (Newton Abbot, 1974) include material on the administration of the old Poor Law. The problem of valuation for rating in the nineteenth and twentieth centuries is examined in J. R. Hicks *et al.*, *The Problem of Valuation for Rating* (Cambridge, 1944). Histories of individual places usually mention local rating, and some of these can be found cited in the notes to this book.

Plenty of scope is available for the local historian who is interested in taxation affairs. Little has been published on the subject, although one interesting study of parish assessments is E. O. Payne's *Property in Land in South Bedfordshire 1750–1832* (Bedfordshire Historical Record Society, xxiii, 1946). The volumes of the *Victoria County History* have generally proved disappointing. My own studies of Cumberland and Westmorland (cited in the notes) have shown the possibilities for studying different counties. I was able to show how the procedures employed in the two counties (the purvey in Cumberland, and the book of rates in Westmorland) worked and of the use to which they were put, the divisions through the counties, and the problem of assessment (both in terms of jurisdiction, and disputed assessments at parish, constablewick and individual level). Similar studies are possible for other counties, since most of the evidence was drawn from quarter sessions records. A number of volumes of such records, for different parts of the country, have been published by local record societies, but these touch only the surface of the material to be found in county record offices. The methods of assessing and collecting within the parish can be studied from petitions to sessions and the orders from sessions (usually found in the order books), together with churchwardens' and vestry papers. Rate books only occasionally shed light on the methods of assessment and collection.

National taxes have received rather more attention, although largely from an overall point of view rather than by specific county and regional studies.

1. **Ship Money.** M. D. Gordon, 'The Collection of Ship Money in the Reign of Charles I', *Trans. R. Hist. Soc.*, 3rd series, vol. iv (1911).

2. **Hearth Tax.** L. M. Marshall, 'The Levying of the Hearth Tax, 1662–1688', *Eng. Hist. Rev.* li (1936); C. A. F. Meekings (ed.), *Dorset Hearth Tax Assessments 1662–4* (Dorchester, 1951); C. A. F. Meekings (ed.), *Surrey Hearth Tax, 1664* (Surrey Record Society xvii, 1940); E. Powell, 'The Hearth Taxes for the Town of Cambridge, A.D. 1664 and 1674', *Cambridge Antiquarian Society Proceedings and Communications* xx (1915); M. M. B. Weinstock (ed.), *Hearth Tax Returns, Oxfordshire, 1665* (Oxfordshire Record Society, xxi, 1940); R. Welford, 'Newcastle Householders in 1665: Assessment of Hearth or Chimney Tax', *Archaeologia Aeliana*, 3rd series, vii (1910).

Good examples of their use for population and social structure are, W. G. Hoskins, *Industry, Trade and People in Exeter* (1935); G. C. Forster, 'York in the Seventeenth Century', in C. M. Tillott (ed.), *V.C.H. City of York* (1961).

3. **Poll Tax. Marriage, Birth and Burials Tax.** P. E. Jones, 'Local Assesments for Parliamentary Taxes', *Journal of the Society of Archivists*, iv (1970).

4. **Land Tax.** W. R. Ward, *The English Land Tax in the Eighteenth Century* (Oxford, 1953). On the advantages and disadvantages of using Land Tax assessments see the following: A. H. Johnson, *The Disappearance of the Small Landowner* (Oxford, 1909, new edition 1963); J. D. Chambers, 'Enclosure and the Small Landowner', *Ec. Hist. Rev.* x (1940); E. Davies, 'The Small Landowner, 1780–1832 in the light of the Land Tax Assessments', *Ec. Hist.*

Rev. i (1927); D. B. Grigg, 'The Land Tax Returns', *Agric. Hist. Rev.* xi (1963); H. G. Hunt, 'Landownership and Enclosure, 1750–1830', *Ec. Hist. Rev.*, 2nd series, xi (1958–9); J. M. Martin, 'Landownership and the Land Tax Returns', *Agric. Hist. Rev.* XIV (1966); G. E. Mingay, 'The Land Tax Assessments and the Small Landowner', *Ec. Hist. Rev.*, 2nd series, xvii (1964).

5. **Window Tax.** W. R. Ward, 'The Administration of the Window and Assessed Taxes, 1696–1798', *Eng. Hist. Rev.* lxvii (1952).

6. **Assessed Taxes** (18th century). J. E. D. Binney, *British Public Finance and Administration, 1774–1792* (Oxford, 1958).

Few of these sources have much to say about the application of local procedures for collecting taxes to national assessments (perhaps because, although widely accepted, this practice was strictly speaking illegal by the terms of the legislation authorising the act). The papers of a receiver-general of taxes will often shed considerable light on how national assessments were levied. Unfortunately, few land tax commissioners' papers survive.

Plenty of opportunity exists to study the administration of taxation at the local level, although no one body of material provides all the answers. A good deal of information can be derived from private correspondence, and from stray official documents surviving by chance among family papers, but few county record offices appear to be aware of just how much material they have on the subject. Consequently the researcher is likely to find relevant material in a whole series of classes, and this renders the task fairly formidable. Hopefully such a warning will not act as a deterrent to anyone interested in the subject. Local taxation deserves to be more thoroughly studied because of the light it sheds on the working of local government.

NOTES
(Place of publication given when other than London.)
1. E. Cannan, *The History of Local Rates in England* (1896), p. 10.
2. 43 Eliz. cap. 2.
3. 14 Car. II cap. 12. S & B Webb, *The Parish and the County* (1963 reprint), p. 216. E. MacKenzie, *An Historical, Topographical and Descriptive View of the County of Northumberland* (2nd ed. Newcastle upon Tyne, 1825), i, p. 242. J. V. Beckett, 'Westmorland's Book of Rates', *Trans. Cumberland & Westmorland*

Antiqu. & Archaeol. Soc. lxxvii (1977), p. 129. Staffordshire R[ecord] O[ffice] Q/SO vol. ii, 1706–19, unfoliated.

4. D. Marshall, *The English Poor in the Eighteenth Century* (1926), p. 83. G. W. Oxley, *Poor Relief in England and Wales 1601–1834* (Newton Abbot, 1974), pp. 49–50. *Report from the Select Committee of the House of Lords appointed to Consider the Laws Relating to Parochial Assessments* (1850), p. 61.

5. 3 Wil. & Mary cap. 11, cl. xi. 17 Geo. II cap. 3, cap. 38. E. O. Payne, *Property in Land in South Bedfordshire 1750–1832* (Bedfordshire Historical Record Society, xxiii, 1946), p. 15. 41 Geo. III cap. 23.

6. S. C. Ratcliffe and H. C. Johnson (eds), *Warwickshire County Records* (Warwick, 1935 ff), i, p. 135.

7. L. M. Marshall, 'The Levying of the Hearth Tax 1662–1688', *Eng. Hist. Rev.* li (1936), pp. 628–46.

8. S. & B. Webb, *The Manor and the Borough* (1924), p. 704. J. Thirsk and J. P. Cooper (eds), *Seventeenth Century Economic Documents* (Oxford, 1972), pp. 620–1. G. Parsloe (ed.), *The Minute Book of Bedford Corporation 1647–64* (Bedfordshire Historical Record Society, xxvi, 1949), pp. 176–7.

9. *Report of the Poor Law Commissioners on Local Taxation* (1843), pp. 22–3. D. Marshall, *The English Poor*, pp. 80, 82. E. Cannan, *History of Local Rates*, ch. IV. A. Redford, *The History of Local Government in Manchester*, i (1939), pp. 179–80. 3 & 4 Vict. cap. 89.

10. Ratcliffe and Johnson, *op. cit.*, i, pp. 38–9. Kendal R.O. D/Ry Box 32, 'Some remarks upon the description of Westmorland by Jo Adams Esq'. W. G. Hoskins, *The Midland Peasant* (1957), pp. 205–10. Staffordshire R.O. D590/327.

11. S. O. Addy, 'The Church Wall at Norton as a Measure of Taxation', *Journal of the Derbyshire Archaeological and Natural History Society* xxxviii (1916), pp. 105–6. Ratcliffe and Johnson, *op. cit.*, ii, pp. 13, 255. D. E. Howell James (ed.), *Norfolk Quarter Sessions Order Book 1650–57* (Norfolk Record Society, xxvi, 1955), p. 81. E. H. Bates (ed.), *Quarter Sessions Records for the County of Somerset Vol. IV 1666–77* (Somerset Record Society, xxxiv, 1919), p. 37. S. A. Peyton (ed.), *Minutes of Proceedings in Quarter Sessions held for the Parts of Kesteven in the County of Lincoln 1674–1695* (Lincoln Record Society, xxvi, 1931), p. 482.

12. Ratcliffe and Johnson, *op. cit.*, i, p. 249, vii, pp. 15, 20. J. Wake (ed.), *Quarter Sessions Records of the County of Northampton-shire 1630, 1657, 1657-8* (Northamptonshire Record Society, i, 1924), p. 187.
13. *A Treatise on Parish Rates* (1764), pp. 17ff.
14. Durham R.O. Q/S/OB/8 1700-32, f.499. 6 & 7 Wil. IV cap. 96, cl. I.
15. E. Cannan, *History of Local Rates*, p. 14. 31 & 32 Vict. cap. 109. W. Albert, *The Turnpike Road System in England 1663-1840* (Cambridge, 1972), p. 16.
16. 23 Hen. VIII cap. 2. 12 Geo. II cap. 29, cl. XI.
17. C. D. Chandaman, *The English Public Revenue 1660-1688* (Oxford, 1975), ch. 5. W. R. Ward, *The English Land Tax in the Eighteenth Century* (Oxford, 1953), pp. 2-3. John Rylands Library, Manchester, Legh of Lyme MSS, Thomas Swettenham to Peter Legh, 17 Nov. 1690. Warwickshire R.O. CR.1028. J. V. Beckett, 'Local Custom and the "New Taxation" of the Seventeenth and Eighteenth Centuries: the Example of Cumberland', *Northern History*, xii (1976), pp. 114-5. J. V. Beckett, 'Westmorland', pp. 129-30.
18. W. G. Hoskins, *The Midland Peasant*, pp. 209-10. E. Cannan, *History of Local Rates*, pp. 4-5.
19. J. Nicolson and R. Burn, *Antiquities and History of the Counties of Westmorland and Cumberland* (1777), i, p. 13. E. Cannan, *History of Local Rates*, pp. 18-20. J. Tait (ed.), *Lancashire Quarter Sessions Records I 1590-1606* (Chetham Society, lxxvii, 1917), p. 164.
20. *Returns Relating to County Rates* (1832). Except where stated otherwise material in the following paragraphs is taken from this report.
21. Carlisle R.O. D/Lons/L, Survey lists, Ravenstonedale bundle 5.
22. Lancashire R.O. DDN/1/64, DDX/603/1. J. Tait (ed.), *Taxation in Salford Hundred 1524-1802* (Chetham Society, lxxxiii, 1924), p. xxxi.
23. Carlisle R.O. D/Lons/L Historical and Legal Records (Extracts 1626-36). Sheffield Central Library, Copley MSS CD 510/1. F. Barber, 'On the Book of Rates for the West Riding of the County of York', *The Yorkshire Archaeological and Topographical Journal* i (1870), pp. 153-68.
24. British Library, Harleian MSS 1920. J. V. Beckett, 'Local

Custom', pp. 107–9. J. Jolley, *The Head Constable's Assistant or, a Mize Book for the County Palatine of Chester* (1726). *A General Rate for the County of Norfolk* (Norwich, 1743).

25. Warwickshire R.O. CR.1028.
26. C[ommons] J[ournal] lxvii (1812), p. 35.
27. J. V. Beckett, 'Westmorland', p. 132. Durham University, Grey MSS vol. 6, f.372. Durham R.O. Q/OB 6 1669–82, f.386. Northumberland R.O. Q.S.O.B. 1687–97, f.12. F. Barber, 'On the Book of Rates', p. 154.
28. C.J. lxvii (1812), p. 35. A. Redford, *The History of Local Government*, i, p. 180.
29. Public R.O. T/1/83, fos. 348, 359. British Library Stowe MSS 747, f.91. *Yorkshire Diaries and Autobiographies* (Surtees Society, lxxvii, Durham, 1886), p. 80.
30. J. V. Beckett, 'Local Custom', pp. 110–11, 'Westmorland', p. 128. C.J. xxiii (1737–41), pp. 217, 289–90. 12 Geo. II cap. 29.
31. Hertfordshire R.O. Carrard MSS 293. S. & B. Webb, *The Parish and the County*, p. 528. Staffordshire R.O. Q/SO vol. 14 1737–50, fos. 58v–59.
32. 24 Geo. III cap. 54, 4 Geo. IV cap. 63. S. & B. Webb, *The Manor and the Borough*, pp. 703–4. Sir Francis Hill, *Georgian Lincoln* (Cambridge, 1966), p. 241. F. Vigier, *Change and Continuity* (1970), pp. 55–7.
33. G. Oxley, *Poor Relief in England and Wales*, pp. 21–3. C. Gill, *History of Birmingham* i (Oxford, 1952), p. 149. A. T. Patterson, *A History of Southampton 1700–1914* i (Southampton Record Series, xi, 1966), pp. 17, 36,
34. G. Bush, *Bristol and its Municipal Government 1820–51* (Bristol Record Society, xxix, 1976), pp. 13, 183. B. D. White, *A History of the Corporation of Liverpool 1835–1914* (Liverpool, 1951), pp. 12–14. A. Redford, *A History of Local Government*, i, pp. 179–80. F. Vigier, *Change and Continuity*, pp. 108–9, 187ff.
35. Charles D'Avenant, 'An Essay upon Ways and Means', in *Works* (C. Whitworth, ed., 1771), i, p. 56.
36. Staffordshire R.O. D1744/52, letter dated 25 Mar 1667. J. V. Beckett, 'Local Custom', p. 114, 'Westmorland', p. 131. Carlisle R.O. D/Lons/W, James Lowther to William Gilpin, 24 Feb 1712/13. Kendal R.O. D/Ry 4289, Sir Daniel Fleming to Sir Christopher Musgrave, 28 Mar 1692.
37. B. E. V. Sabine, *A History of Income Tax* (1966), ch. 1. F.

Shehab, *Progressive Taxation* (Oxford, 1953), ch. 2. S. Dowell, *A History of Taxation and Taxes in England* (3rd edition, 1965), iii, pp. 92ff.

38. *Gentleman's Magazine* xiv (1744), pp. 654–7, xxxv (1765), pp. 157–8.
39. S. C. Ratcliffe and H. C. Johnson, *Warwickshire County Records*, ii, pp. 23, 162. E. O. Payne, *Property in Land*, pp. 19, 34.
40. E. Moir, *Local Government in Gloucestershire 1775–1800* (Bristol and Gloucestershire Archaeological Society Records Section, viii, 1969), pp. 97–8, 106.
41. B. Keith-Lucas, *English Local Government in the Nineteenth and Twentieth Centuries* (1977), p. 7. S. & B. Webb, *The Parish and the County*, p. 595. *Statutory Authorities for Special Purposes* (1922), p. 407. W. Holdsworth, *A History of English Law*, x (1938), p. 338.
42. *Returns Relating to County Rates* (1832), p. 151. 49 Geo. III cap. 139. D. Marshall, *The English Poor*, pp. 85, 246.
43. 37 Geo. III cap. 65. 44 Geo. III cap. xxxiv. 47 Geo. III cap. xxxiv. 50 Geo. III cap. i. 53 Geo. III cap. lxxvii. 54 Geo. III cap. ciii. J. V. Beckett, 'Local Custom', p. 129. S. & B. Webb, *The Parish and the County*, p. 428.
44. J. Thrupp, 'Devon Quarter Sessions 1800–30' (unpublished Birmingham University thesis, 1950), pp. 38–40. C.J. lxvii (1812), pp. 35, 101, 103, lxviii (1812/13), pp. 96, 123, 133, 428. *Gentleman's Magazine* lxxxii pt. 2 (1812), p. 421, lxxxiii pt. 2 (1813), pp. 318–9, 352, 550.
45. S. & B. Webb, *The Parish and the County*, p. 141.
46. *Gentleman's Magazine* lxxx (1810), p. 23. 52 Geo. III cap. 110.
47. S. Dowell, *A History of Taxation*, pp. 92–105.
48. 55 Geo. III cap. 51.
49. 56 Geo. III cap. 49. 57 Geo. III cap. 94. 1 & 2 Geo. IV cap. 85.
50. *Returns Relating to County Rates* (1832). *Report of the Poor Law Commissioners on Local Taxation* (1843), pp. 33–4.
51. Lancashire R.O. QSG/1/1 fos. 210–11. P. Styles, *The Development of County Administration in the late XVIII and early XIXth Centuries* (Oxford, Dugdale Society, 1934), p. 26. J. V. Beckett, 'Westmorland', p. 134.
52. Devon R.O. Petition from Washford Pyne, Michaelmas 1815. J. Thrupp, 'Devon Quarter Sessions', pp. 39–40.
53. W. E. Tate, *The Parish Chest* (Cambridge, 1946), p. 29. *Report*

from the Select Committee of the House of Lords . . . into the charges of the County Rates in England and Wales (1835), pp. 320ff. *Report from the Select Committee on County Rates* (1834), pp. 30ff.

54. *Ibid.*, pp. vii, xi, 28. *Report of the Commissioners for Inquiring into County Rates and other matters therewith* (1836), p. 4. *Report from the Select Committee of the House of Lords* (1835), pp. 7–8.

55. *Ibid*, p. iii. B. Keith-Lucas, *English Local Government*, p. 7.

56. Memorandum of Sir E. W. Hamilton to the *Royal Commission on Local Taxation* (1898–1902), Parliamentary Papers 1899, xxxvi 685. *Report from the Select Committee on the Expenditure of County Rates* (1825), p. 3. *Report of the Poor Law Commissioners* (1843).

57. *Report of the Select Committee to inquire into the Assessment and Collection of Poor Rates and other Local Rates and Taxes* (1868), p. iii. *Report from the Select Committee on Local Taxation* (1870), p. iv. W. Rathbone, *Local Government and Taxation in England and Wales* (1883), pp. 2–4, 16.

58. G. Bush, *Bristol and its Municipal Government*, p. 183.

59. 6 & 7 Wil. IV cap. 103. 12 & 13 Vict. cap. 65.

60. 3 & 4 Vict. cap. 89. 37 & 38 Vict. cap. 54. W. Holdsworth, *A History of English Law* x, pp. 286–7.

61. *Report from the Select Committee of the House of Lords* (1850), pp. 3ff, 147, 325–35. G. L. Hutchinson, *A Plan for the Equalization of the Poor Rates* (1849).

62. 25 & 26 Vict. cap. 109. 28 & 29 Vict. cap. 79.

63. 32 & 33 Vict. cap. 67. J. R. Hicks, J. K. Hicks and C. E. V. Leser, *The Problem of Valuation for Rating* (Cambridge, 1944), pp. 20–1. *Report of the Rt. Hon. G. J. Goshen MP . . . to the Rt. Hon. the Lords Commissioners of Her Majesty's Treasury on the Progressive Increase of Local Taxation* (1870). W. Rathbone, *Local Government and Taxation*, pp. 2, 11, *Local Government and Taxation* (1875), pp. 6, 10. *Royal Commission on Local Taxation* (1898–1902).

64. G. Oxley, *Poor Relief in England and Wales*, p. 49. 3 & 4 Wil. IV cap. 90, 13 & 14 Vict. cap. 99. D. Ashworth, 'The Urban Poor Law', in D. Fraser (ed.), *The New Poor Law in the Nineteenth Century* (1976), pp. 142–3. 33 Vict. cap. 41. W. Rathbone, *Local Taxation and Poor Law Administration in Great Cities* (1869), quoted in M. Rose (ed.), *The English Poor Law* (Newton Abbot, 1971), p. 220.

65. 15 & 16 Geo. V cap. 19.